F*ck You, 2016

# F*ck You, 2016

*An homage to a year of unparalleled cockhattery, fuckmuppetry and shitcombobulating world events*

BOB A. N. GRYPANTS

MICHAEL JOSEPH
*an imprint of*
PENGUIN BOOKS

MICHAEL JOSEPH

UK | USA | Canada | Ireland | Australia
India | New Zealand | South Africa

Michael Joseph is part of the Penguin Random House group of companies
whose addresses can be found at global.penguinrandomhouse.com.

First published in Great Britain by Michael Joseph 2016
002

Set in 11.75/14 pt Garamond MT Std
Typeset by Jouve (UK), Milton Keynes
Printed in Great Britain by Clays Ltd, St Ives plc

A CIP catalogue record for this book is available from the British Library

ISBN: 978-0-718-18774-3


www.greenpenguin.co.uk

Penguin Random House is committed to a
sustainable future for our business, our readers
and our planet. This book is made from Forest
Stewardship Council® certified paper.

# Contents

# Introduction

Welcome! Sit down. Make a cup of tea. Get yourself comfortable. You deserve a break. It's been a trumptastically shit-awful year, replete with so many terrible events, deaths, cock-ups and miscellaneous shittery that you'd be forgiven for wanting to leave planet Earth altogether. But worry not – for this book is here to offer a consoling pat on the shoulder, a gentle nudge towards a hopefully brighter vista ahead. Yes, this year has been terrible, but is it the *worst* year *ever*? Let's find out! We'll remind ourselves just how arse-breakingly awful much of this year has been, whether it's in the field of politics or the economy or simply the general nonsense of everyday life, before looking at awful years throughout history. How bad can things get? We'll ask whether we did something naughty in 2015 to deserve all this fuckmuppetry, and look at whether next year might be another dreadful year. We'll also ask whether there's been *anything* good to happen this year and . . . There has! We'll show you!

The core message of the book is 'don't feel alone'. The rage and bewilderment which you may feel pent up inside is mirrored in these pages. It's been a continuous accretion of terrible stuff, one thing after another, but we've been through it together. So let this book be a companion; one which may provide a small measure of catharsis. And once you've read it, on 31 December, if not before, throw this book in the bin and forget about it. Along with the year as a whole. Best thing for it.

Come, gentle reader, let's voyage back into the world that is and was 2016 . . .

# The context: did we do something naughty in 2015?

Inevitably, when faced with a giant shit-bomb of a year like the one we've had, it makes sense to ask the question, did we do something wrong? Have we somehow deserved a year of such relentless misery? Asking this assumes a certain degree of cosmological order to the universe which 2016 might sadly have proven is, quite simply, *not there* (or that David Bowie was actually holding the fabric of the universe together). Yet such a startling confluence of crap – and, let's be honest, we've waded through so much of it that it has been like going for a swim in the central reservoir of a gigantic sewage system – begs the question of whether it's just a coincidence or is there some universal Karmic balancing act in train.

Well, let's look at 2015. The Paris Agreement on climate change was reached, marking a major step forward in controlling emissions, whilst Russia meanwhile entered into the Syrian civil war, vastly complicating an already terrible mess of a situation; positive negotiations were concluded on Iran's nuclear program, yet ISIS terrorists launched attacks on three separate continents; corruption within FIFA, world football's governing body, was finally addressed and rooted out, but the world faced the start of a growing refugee crisis; Cuba and the USA restored diplomatic ties, yet Volkswagen was accused of cheating on diesel emissions tests. (Herbie, how *could* you?) Verily, 2015 was a year of two halves: one shit, the other pretty good. It was a *balanced* year. It had its fair share of ups and downs – perhaps no more than normal. Cosmologically, it felt ok . . . Certainly not so out of the ordinary that we'd feel understanding and accepting towards the mayhem of 2016.

No, it seems that out of the blue we've been hit by a relentless deluge of comet-sized turds for no other reason than . . . COINCIDENCE.

And in a swirling universe that is characterized by chaos and chance, this is perhaps the best explanation we can hope for. We've just been really, really unlucky. So let us not look for mollifying explanations or consolatory causes – let us instead embrace the chaos for what it is; having been kicked in the groin by an uncaring universe, let's stand tall, square up to our faceless enemy and smile back into the abyss.

*Hint: we're just about to leap over the edge and into the abyss.*

# Politics and politicians

Well, let's face it. We don't know who we are any more, do we? Up until June this year we were British and more or less considered ourselves to be one nation. There appeared to be a shared set of beliefs and values; we all (or at least most of us) liked Gary Lineker; we had no reason to be suspicious of our own grandparents; and the notion that the political views of another part of the country might be diametrically opposed to our own didn't cross our minds. But look at Gary Lineker now! Division has occurred and even our sometime national football captain is drawn into the vortex of it. Back in 1859, the liberal philosopher J. S. Mill argued that a progressive society must allow for and encourage diversity of opinion – without it, he suggested, society would stagnate and tend towards autocracy, a lack of originality and an increase in general levels of stupidity. But could he have foreseen a UK with an almost even split down its middle, with those caught on either side deeply, vehemently sceptical about the others' views? A country where young and old have begun to feel totally odds with one another? Could he fuck.

## *A fucking fiasco of a referendum*

Like a car with no brakes hurtling towards a cliff, many in the UK felt a degree of reluctance towards what lay ahead when the referendum was announced. The glib confidence with which David Cameron ploughed on behind the wheel, assured that it would cement his reputation as the man who saw off the irritating question of EU membership once and for all, had a calming effect on many who might otherwise have thought, 'Oh, fuck' . . . The irony is that many people *didn't* want a referendum. Lesson for the future? Let's hold referendums about having referendums. What people were perhaps most unprepared for was the shock. The oh-shit-this-is-really-happening moment. The morning-after shame, guilt and remorse. Half the nation had the result they wanted (or thought they wanted) whereas half the nation was distraught. No wonder, then, that a petition begging for a second referendum was soon set up, attracting millions of signatures in a matter of days. And then came the realization that many who had voted had done so based on a slim if not nonexistent grasp of the consequences. You mean, we won't be able to travel and work in European countries? We might not actually be able to take control of our borders? MARMITE PRICES MIGHT GO UP????? Like finding oneself pregnant after a throwaway one night stand, many

4

voters were furious at themselves and their government for leading them, inexorably, into the path of choice. Britain had voted for Brexit!!

## FUCKING BREXIT

The big one. The grand shitcombobulation of a once proud country. After the threat of Grexit and the spectre of Frexit, Spexit and Whateverthefuckelseexit, here was something real and tangible. And happening to us! A real exit! OR WAS IT? Article 50, like Area 51, was an all but unknown, distant and enigmatic concept until it became an ever-present topic of debate. But who would be debating its influence on whether or not the dream/nightmare would become a reality? Well, David Cameron somehow managed to leap out of the car with a grin on his face, just as it zoomed into space ... And so, leaderless, we plunged downwards. Which can only have led to:

### *The leadership battle*

It's very hard to look back now and believe that the convoluted mess that followed the referendum result really took place, with such an array of fuckwittery contending for the Tory leadership. Were we really so close to having Michael Gove as its lord and master?

REALLY? Let's just remind ourselves how it unfolded, with all the grace and decorum of a well-groomed turnip.

First, in the wake of the worst hangover 48 per cent of the nation had ever experienced, two frontrunners emerged: Boris Johnson and Theresa May. The terrifying possibility of a Bojo government was tantalisingly close at hand . . . the stars were aligning . . . only for a giant spanner to be thrown into his plans. With the deft and sudden violence of a stealth bomber, Michael Gove, a key ally to Boris, announced that he had thought long and hard and had reluctantly come to the conclusion that, after all, Boris could not 'provide the leadership or build the team for the task ahead'. *Et tu, Michael?* Would this political assassination clear the way for a sprint finish to the premiership? No.

Five candidates boldly stepped forward to offer their services to the nation, entering the ballot with varying levels of probability surrounding their potential success: Stephen Crabb, Michael Gove, Liam Fox, Angela Leadsom and Theresa May. May came out top, followed by Leadsom; Fox was eliminated; Crabb withdrew (both Fox and Crabb lent their support to May); and Gove, meanwhile, ploughed on, empowered by the natural charisma of a lukewarm fromage frais. The second ballot saw Gove placed third, eliminating him from the race. Did he mind? Seemingly not. As he put it, creating levity out of the situation, 'We have now reached the point where everyone can be a candidate for prime minister for fifteen minutes. And boy were those fifteen minutes fun . . .' Ha ha. You broccoli-brained arsenit.

Then Angela Leadsom, thanks to a somewhat misguided suggestion that being a parent was in some way a prerequisite to successful governance, managed to annihilate her own chances, even despite having a team of her suporters march down Whitehall wearing slogan-bearing T-shirts over suits and chanting, 'What do we want? Leadsom for leader. When do we want it? Now!' The sort of cringe-worthy sight that automatically makes your bum muscles clench. Not unlike the legendary 1968 Golden Globe Race, the non-stop, single-handed, round-the-world yacht race, when half the competitors pulled out before leaving the Atlantic, one sank, another committed suicide and another decided to simply keep on sailing. There realistically could only be one winner – the last person standing.

## *Theresa fucking May*

Apart from looking like a mischievous squirrel who's just uncovered a cache of nuts, and having a loudly proclaimed fondness for shoes, May still seems a somewhat unknown quantity to the British electorate. And given that we didn't vote for her this is perhaps unsurprising. How will she manage the fraught and challenging road ahead? Do we trust her? Do we like her? Do we have any choice in the matter?

We also now have May to thank for 'Spreadsheet Phil' and his obsession with jam. It's all he talks about. Someone get the guy some breakfast! It's distracting him from the serious business of managing our post-Brexit national debt, set to reach £1,950,198,032,349 by 2021. Less jam, more pie, calculated to 13 digits. Phil, who apparently ran glam rock discos in his youth and dressed as a goth, now looks more like a stunt double for Peter Cushing, gearing up to pay a trip to Dartmouth to hunt down that pesky Baskerville hound. Not now, Phil! Get to work on the spreadsheet!

Meanwhile, poor Mark Carney looks more and more like a man who's struggling to control a belligerent classroom menace and who is on the verge of giving up and saying *fuck it, you run the lesson*. Let's hope he doesn't. We need experts! We need a cabinet full of qualified, able men and women who have a calling and vocation for their portfolio! A natural suitability! We need . . .

## *Boris Johnson as foreign secretary*

Yes. The ultimate joke has been played. Not just on Boris but on the nation. I know, let's put the one individual least qualified to bring about peace and accord in a time of tumultuous discord into a position where he can really fuck things up! As a bit of a joke! You know, to get him back for all the silly comments and to scupper his leadership ambitions! As a punishment for backing the wrong horse. Forget about the impact on the country! Yes, that's right. Like an Aryan man-child born of Richmal Crompton's imagination, complete with charmingly tousled hair, the giant human blancmange that is Boris Johnson has now entered the international arena of foreign policy – not unlike a kid in a Swiss clock factory carrying a bag of spanners, joyously begging to start toying with anything that looks complicated and mechanical. Let loose like a violent fart in an elevator, or a turbo-charged Duke of Edinburgh, he has happily subverted centuries of diplomatic practice and protocol in a blatant and helpless attempt to emulate his intellectual hero Churchill with his witticisms, yet has come across more like Alan Partridge at a funeral: Aha! I just said bollocks in Hungarian! Watch me, watch me, as I characterize the Italians as a prosecco-producing nation of fools, desperate to get their hands on our much-sought-after fish and chips! Bumbling Bojo looks set to remain in his position for some time to come. At least long enough to truly embarrass an entire nation.

It's enough to make one almost nostalgic for the early days of Cameron's reign. Almost.

## *David fucking Cameron*

Last year we found out that ex-Prime Minister David Cameron did or did not shag a severed pig's head. This year he instigated a referendum and the side which he backed lost, costing him his job and those of nearly all his friends in government. Despite all of the above, the pig has kept a dignified silence. Let's also just remind ourselves that Big Dave once famously said, with charming whimsy, about his forthcoming incumbency, 'How hard can it be?' Git.

But enough about us. Look! Something's happening over there! No, wait, it can't be . . . Surely not?

## *Donald Fucking Trump*

The unthinkable has happened twice in one year. Like lightning made out of electrified shit striking twice. The hair made out of shredded wheat! The fake tan! The staggering misogyny! Yes, The Donald has become president of the Free World.

Trump became president-elect in 2016 for one reason only: he turned the democratic election of the most powerful country in the western world into a reality

TV show. Unfortunately, it's now a reality the rest of us must all live in. After coming to the conscious attention of most of the world through his appearances on *The Apprentice* – where a group of younger, swivel-eyed narcissists attempt to impress and gain employment with the swivel-eyed narcissist in chief – it really was little wonder that Donald Trump himself would eventually think about running for the world's most high-profile job.

And how did he go about it?

By doing what every successful, fame-hungry reality TV star has ever done to stay in the race: act up for the camera, show off unashamedly, pick on the other candidates' weaknesses, be outrageous (and unrepentant to the outraged), and when finally caught with their pants down, wave it about a bit so that everyone is too embarrassed to bring up the subject ever again. Is it any wonder that the spectacle-loving media and the confused voters loved him? They could no longer distinguish between reality and a reality TV show scripted in the editing room. Voters just thought this was *The Apprentice* with a much bigger budget, fewer participants, a more grueling format and fewer advertisers to upset when things turned really nasty.

And how did it end?

In reality TV, everyone votes for the most entertaining candidate. And it turns out they do the same in reality too. *Fuck*.

Expect reality's ratings to go through the roof for the next four years.

## *Donald Trump's Hair*

Not since the glory days of *Dallas* and *Dynasty* has so much hair spray been used on just one hairpiece. No wonder he blames global warning on a Chinese conspiracy! He's trying to divert attention from the fact that he's single-handedly responsible for it. I mean, it doesn't even look like human hair. It more resembles a collection of wispily ginger plastic fronds, the kind you'd find rooted to the bottom of an aquarium at the bloody dentist's.

Even the laws of physics break down in its general vicinity. If there's a breeze, it sort of moves at right angles to the prevailing wind direction, as if it is trying to crawl down the back of Trump's head (or do us all a favour and hide his face). These independent movements have led some to speculate that the hair is not in actual fact real. Instead, they believe, it is the spindly, wisp-like body of some alien intelligence which has parasitically attached itself to Trump's head and has taken over the miniscule brain residing inside. This then explains the repellant narcissism of his every utterance, his domineering voice, the contempt with which the man clearly views most of humanity and why he is now in control of the world's largest strategic nuclear arsenal.

The only hope we perhaps have that our new alien overlord will not destroy us in fit of pique is that it has not reckoned on the weakness of Trump's little, little hands. These may not actually be strong enough to push the big 'Nuclear is Go' button in the Oval Office, if it should come to a full-on strike against *The New York Times* or some other offender deserving of the president's full wrath.

Perhaps that is why Trump chose as his vice president Mike 'Hands Like Dinner Plates' Pence. A man by the way, who proclaims evolution to be just a theory.

## *Hillary Clinton*

It's just sad, really, isn't it?

Many of us, while contemplating the smoking wreckage that is the US presidential election result, have wondered aloud, 'Was this really about racism, or sexism? (Or economic anxiety? Or covert manipulation of the electoral system by a hostile foreign power?)' A pertinent series of questions to which the answer is, of course, 'yes'.

But let's focus, just for a few nauseating moments, on the *sexism*.

You may not be a fan of Hillary Rodham Clinton. Good for you. Your medal for fearless iconoclasm is doubtless in the post. Perhaps you suspect her of corruption; perhaps you even have *evidence* of her wrongdoing (although if you do, you appear to have made the puzzling decision to keep it a secret from all the world's press and the FBI).

Perhaps you're an IT professional whose own use of email scrupulously adheres to best practice, and who is so offended by Hillary's decision to use a private server that you would sooner hand control of the most fearsome arsenal of extinction-threatening weaponry ever assembled by man to a fatuous spray-tanned Mussolini than see a highly-qualified woman who has the impertinence to wear *trousers* assume a position of political power . . .

Is Hillary Clinton stereotypically a career politician? Yes. Is she a friend of bankers, and very fond of money? Clearly. Has she supported military adventures abroad, and illiberal policies at home? Yes – among other things – she has. But is *any* of the foregoing *remotely* unusual among her male peers in Washington? No, it is not.

It is a common form of sexism to hold women to far higher standards (of behaviour, of appearance, of integrity) than their male counterparts. In the US presidential election of 2016 we saw a woman held to absurdly, impossibly high standards, while the man she ran against was literally held to *no standards at all.*

That is sexism, at its jaw-dropping, soul-crushing worst.

Meanwhile, back in the UK, many of the voting public were coming to terms with the reality of having a government with no effective opposition . . .

## *Jeremy fucking Corbyn*

To many, he's been a saviour. He's ushered in a promise of a new man-of-the-people era in politics, true left wing values and a genuine ideological counter to the Tories. And yet . . . and yet . . . like his greying vest gradually revealing itself underneath that pallid yellow shirt, Corbyn's Stalinist ambition and demonstrable inability to unite rather than divide a riven party have become increasingly obvious. We can forgive him for not singing the nation anthem; we can forgive the lack of humour, humility and statesmanship; but can we forgive him for being a key architect in the erosion of the political centre left? If you think he's brought in a new, kinder style of politics then think again. Or just ask anyone who has had bricks thrown through their windows. The violence, intimidation and narrow-minded fanaticism shown by some of his followers is just as scary and nauseating as the clown-like behavior of the far right. Jezza is perhaps one of history's best examples of how having a beard whilst in a position of power can confer the illusion of avuncular benevolence. Facial hair can suggest all manner of things, especially in politics. To illustrate the point:

### The Beard

Jeremy Corbyn, sticking it to the 'man'.

*The beard has historically suggested a healthy disregard for human vanity and pretence, and inevitably so, given that its wearers invariably look like scruffbags. It is developed as a look only upon leaving politics (see Al Gore, but also Ed Miliband's notorious 'milibeard'), as if to say, fuck y'all, this is me in all my hirsute glory – you can't tame me! Corbyn has, atypically, opted for a beard throughout his entire political career – one long, persistent, unwavering statement that he really gives no fucks about 'da man'. You stick it to him, Jeremy! Good for you!*

## The Moustache

Nigel Farage , with moustache.
The only blessing was that he didn't grow it in
November.

Classically worn only by fascists and dictators (for example, Robert Mugabe, Enoch Powell, Bashar Hafez al-Assad and – until terrified advisors warned him of its semiotic perils – Nigel Farage), the moustache remains a niche look in mainstream politics – perhaps with good reason: few sane people would opt for a style that looks as though one's face is being assaulted by a hairy leech.

## The Goatee

Benjamin Disraeli, who infamously spent a large proportion of his political career fondling his chin.

*Rare — few people can successfully pull this look off, as it sits uncomfortably between appearing contrived and relaxed. More successful was the chin-only-goatee, which was worn with great effect by Benjamin Disraeli.*

## The Porkchop

William Ewart Gladstone , who ,
during his maiden speech in parliament,
announced that he would be "bringing sexy back."

*This is a Real Man's facial hair. It almost suggests that one's testosterone levels are so high that hair is inexorably sprouting from one's ears. A fierce, determined and stately look. Due to make a comeback, this author believes, at the next presidential election in 2020. Watch this space.*

## John McDonnell

There's a suggestion of barely contained fierceness to McDonnell, Corbyn's shadow chancellor, as though he might secretly spend his weekends reenacting the battle scene in *Braveheart*, smeared in blue paint and with only a loincloth to preserve his modesty. Or possibly a reenactment of the miners' strike, complete with charging police horses. He gave us a brilliant moment earlier this year when he pulled out his copy of Chairman Mao's Little Red Book, waving it around manically. What people failed to grasp was that he was actually attempting to inaugurate a new weekly Westminster book group. He'd even lined up Tom Watson to talk about *The Kite Runner* the following week. Sadly, it didn't take off, rather like John Major's ill-fated attempt back in 1990 to introduce a session of 'shag, marry or push off a cliff' into prime minister's question time.

John evidently needs to work on his stagecraft, as demonstrated by a photograph showing the entire backbench fucking about on their phones. Everyone was on twitter, according to John, because 'they were tweeting about what I was saying'. No they weren't, John! They were desperately hunting for an emoji to express their emotional state – something like this:

## *Nigel fucking, fucking, fucking Farage*

There can be few more depressing word-pairings in the English language (although isn't 'Farage' French?). Want to know what's even more depressing? Nigel Farage is the most effective politician of his generation. He has achieved his goals more completely than almost anyone else. He frightened David Cameron into a needless referendum and tricked the country into leaving Europe. He has set the agenda for almost all mainstream politicians since, almost none of whom have the courage to dissent from his pet project. At the time of writing, he is being tipped for the House of Lords.

At least Farage has a sense of humour, as shown by his recent celebrations at the Ritz. With these Ferrero Rocher you're really spoiling us! It's funny because of that old advert! You know, that one where the guy goes 'the ambassador's receptions are noted in society for their host's exquisite taste that captivates his guests' and then a butler brings out a bowl of Ferrero Rocher and that's funny because Mr Trump said you should be ambassador to the US and it's like you're pretending to be an ambassador already because you're eating Ferrero Rocher and having a party like the ambassador but it's not a real one and there's Ferrero Rocher, but not a real ambassador just like the one in the advert but that's funny because it's like you really are an ambassador, oh ha ha ha ha ha, BLEURGHHHHHhhhcccCRACK!! I've just simultaneously vomited and cracked a rib because I was laughing so hard at this masterpiece of referential irony. Oh, you fucking fucking fuck-bucket, Farage! F ffff . . . fff . . . pht [head exploding].

What would Byron, another lord, have to say about Farage? Had he been writing two hundred years later than he did, the great liberal satirist surely would have had a view, perhaps working a few stanzas into *Don Juan*?

Oh great and mighty Farage! O amphibian overlord!
David Icke was right! From the Draco constellation
    comes a race
That threatens to put humanity to the sword
Whilst hiding behind the reassuring posture of
    a smiling face;
Yet in Farage the mask has slipped, he lets fall
    reptilian words,
Whilst beaming bonhomie here, there and all over
    the place.
Like John Bull, red britches swapped for a quotidian suit
    and beefsteak for a pint of pride,
His jovial gurning distracts from a hatred that's never
    articulated, just implied.

But when politics buckles truth and builds escalators
    up cliffs,

Lies about public funding and offers hatred a set of tools,
Encourages foaming rage and fissures and rifts,
I'm reminded sadly of an incident involving a group of
 misguided fools
Who hung a monkey, shipwrecked and scared, that
 fortune had intended as a gift,
The sole survivor of a napoleonic ship, washed ashore
 in Hartlepool.
Put on trial, questioned by a kangaroo court and
 judged a spy,
A silent defendant, unable to laugh, argue, beseech
 or cry.

Would you have been their mayor? Would you have led
 the crowd?
Would you have stood in the midst of them, directing
 their fear?
Would you have watched the clumsy act, grinning
 and proud,
And would you have noticed the animal's terrified tears?
What could a mute beast hope to utter aloud,
What could it say to prolong its years?
The world was reduced to a marketplace, foreign threat to
 a shivering chimpanzee.
As impotent fear found expression in misdirected and
 idiotic cruelty.

It's possible that Nigel Farage may become an ambassador to the US. Trump has stated, with unblinking

confidence, that 'people would like that'. One saving grace could be that Farage may end up being exiled to America – if that happens, we really would be ending 2016 on an up, especially if Bruce Springsteen became Britain's next US ambassador.

That is, unless, the spectre of Tony Blair returning to UK politics to 'sort out the mess' becomes a reality . . .

A rise in populist politics seems to be growing, like a wave. Is that bad, though? What's under threat? Well, possibly a lot. The Holocaust began with words, and it's a very simple leap to go from racist rhetoric to xenophobic policy. Does anyone really think the rise in race-related attacks we've seen is disconnected from the bigger picture? But it's worth remembering what J. S. Mill meant when he wrote about freedom of speech in politics: if you suppress another opinion you simply weaken your own. Or, in his words:

'The peculiar evil of silencing the expression of an opinion is, that it is robbing the human race; posterity as well as the existing generation; those who dissent from the opinion, still more than those who hold it. If the opinion is right, they are deprived of the opportunity of exchanging error for truth: if wrong, they lose, what is almost as great a benefit, the clearer perception and livelier impression of truth, produced by its collision with error.'

No one likes not being listened to, which is one reason we've seen populist revolts against a perceived liberal elite. But at the heart of any liberal thinking should be acceptance and engagement. As Evelyn Beatrice Hall put it, summarizing Voltaire's philosophy, 'I may disapprove of what you say but I will defend to the death your right to say it'. Building bridges, gaining understanding and working with what's happened seems a sensible option. Certainly a better idea than building massive fuck-off walls . . .

# Oh bloody hell, they haven't died TOO, have they?

As I write this, The Starman, the Pop Prince in a raspberry beret, the greatest boxer of all time and Snape, the softly spoken cloak billower, are all together floating down a river of Gene Wilder's chocolate in the sky. These wonderful human beings apparently received a memo for 2016 that the rest of us mere mortals didn't. As we wallow in grief, scowling at our prejudiced aged Aunt who voted to leave Europe, the creative geniuses are high above us having the most interesting dinner party of ALL time in the clouds. Meanwhile we will stockpile bubble wrap and keep a close eye on David Attenborough and Bruce Forsyth.

NB a note of warning: this is a bit sad.

## *Victoria Wood (19 May 1953–20 April 2016)*

One of the funniest women ever to grace the planet, Victoria brought us laughter and tears, in a career that covered writing and acting, drama and comedy. She gave us Acorn Antiques, Dinnerladies and Housewife

49 – and who knows what else she might have gifted to the world? Christmas won't be the same without her.

## *David Bowie*
### *(8 January 1947–10 January 2016)*

How many generations have grown up listening to the music of the Thin White Duke? Ever since the late 60s, Bowie produced boundary-breaking, mesmerizingly beautiful music across an unbelievable range of genres, amassing record sales of 140,000,000. He kept his illness a secret to the end, yet had brilliantly planned the release of a new album – which would still amaze and beguile with its originality. Farewell, Ziggy – and thank you for all the incredible music. Bowie always had an eye on the future – perpaps he saw what was coming in 2016 and decided to make a swift exit.

## *Ronnie Corbett*
### *(4 December 1930–31 March 2016)*

The legendary and very little funny man who, along with Ronnie Barker, brought the world the Two Ronnies and some of the funniest sketches ever committed to celluloid. Who will ever forget his armchair monologues? He was someone you always felt you knew personally, simply due to his warm and irresistible amiability.

## Alan Rickman
### (21 February 1946–14 January 2016)

Truly, simply, tragic. A wonderful actor and, by the sounds of it, a really lovely bloke, who gave us unforgettable performances in the Harry Potter films as well as playing evil baddie Hans Gruber in *Die Hard* and the evil sheriff of Nottingham in *Robin Hood*. He once said, brilliantly, 'I do take my work seriously and the way to do that is not to take yourself too seriously.'

## Paul Daniels
### (6 April 1938–17 March 2016)

The inimitable, lovely man who brought magic to TV screens through the 70s, 80s and 90s. He did bring us Wizbit, a surreal children's TV show about a cone-shaped magician and his friend, Woolly the rabbit, who lived in Puzzleopolis, but let's forgive him for that ... he brought smiles, laughter and a sense of wonder to a generation.

## Terry Wogan
## (3 August 1938–31 January 2016),

If anyone was deserving of the moniker 'national treasure' it was surely Terry. A radio and television broadcasting legend who gave us Wogan and countless years of entertainment as the host of Eurovision (steadily getting more and more legless and increasingly annoyed at the cronyistic voting patterns). Children in Need, which he supported in such a big way for so many years, positively impacted on the lives of a great number of people. His view was that kindness was the most important thing in the world – more so than money or celebrity, for certain. A hero of a man.

## Prince (7 June 1958–21 April 2016)

The legend formerly known as the artist formerly known as Prince, the enigmatically brilliant musical genius who gave us 'Raspberry Beret', 'Little Red Corvette', 'Kiss', and 'Beginning Endlessly' is now gone. If there is a heaven, let's hope that he's dancing like it's 1999 under a cloud of purple rain.

## Leonard Cohen
### (21 September 1934–7 November 2016)

Leonard Cohen, the Canadian singer, songwriter, musician, poet, novelist, philosopher, visionary, friend to the miserable and general comfort to the living sadly passed away on the eve of the US election. Cohen is perhaps best known to people under the age of thirty by his masterpiece, the song 'Hallelujah'. It took him five years to write it – five sodding years! Imagine! And all of three and a half minutes for it to be bastardized, ripped apart and thrown into the cheap, vomit-filled inferno of Simon Cowell's *X-Factor* cauldron. Cohen loved the bleak. He was able to inhabit miserableness so effectively that he was awarded the monikers 'The Godfather of Gloom' and 'The High Priest of Pathos'. He was so beautifully melancholic (if a little bear-baity) that his last album, which he released of course in 2016, was called *You Want It Darker*. 'No!' we all said in reply. 'It can't get any darker! We're sick of the dark – this is worse than Han Solo dying last Christmas!' But it did. And it seems almost fitting that we lost this metaphorical giant in the shittest, most rubbish year in living memory. We should be glad at least that he wasn't around to see Trump win *The Apprentice*. Sorry, I of course mean the American presidential election! Pfft.

### Gene Wilder
### (11 June 1933–29 August 2016)

A comedy and acting legend. If you want to cheer yourself up, watch Blazing Saddles and marvel at his brilliance.

### Johan Cruyff
### (5 April 1947–24 March 2016)

A footballing legend – synonymous with the fabled Cruyff Turn and the introduction of total football.

### Caroline Aherne
### (24 December 1963–2 July 2016)

A comedy legend. The Royle Family! The Mrs Merton show!

### George Martin
### (3 January 1926–8 March 2016)

The record producing legend, composer, arranger, conductor and musician who was known as the 'Fifth Beatle' by none other than Sir Paul McCartney, thanks to the influence and input he had on the band's recordings.

## *Harper Lee*
### *(28 April 1926–19 February 2016)*

A writing legend, who gave us on of the most powerful and inspiring books ever written in the shape of *To Kill a Mockingbird*.

## *Glenn Frey*
### *(6 November 1948–18 January 2016)*

A founding member and frontman of the Eagles. Take it easy, Glenn . . .

## *Muhammad Ali*
### *(17 January 1942–3 June 2016)*

A sporting legend. It seemed he'd never die and it doesn't seem possible he actually did. Ali was possibly the greatest sportsman of the twentieth century. And partly because he wasn't just a sportsman – he was a brave and selfless conscientious objector as well as a champion for racial equality, never shy of expressing and defending his beliefs. He was an amazing boxer and an amazing man.

## *Jo Cox (22 June 1974–16 June 2016)*

This author hopes that referring to something as sad as the murder of Jo Cox in what is meant as an irreverent and silly book won't cause offence. But I'm including her because I think her death was one of the most tragic things to happen this year. And, personally, it was probably the point when I thought to myself, 'really, what the fuck is happening? To our country, to the people in it, to the world?' Jo was a Labour MP from Yorkshire, who had worked as head of policy at Oxfam before winning a seat in the 2015 election. She was shot and stabbed in Birstall by a stranger, a man currently on trial, who shouted 'Britain first' as he attacked her.

That someone as obviously kind, principled and brave as her, a wife and mum of two kids, who campaigned to help vulnerable people in need, should have been brutally killed is awful beyond belief. But more awful still would be forgetting that it happened. That and not feeling compelled, in some small way, to make the world a safer, happier and kinder place.

## *Bill Hicks*
### *(16 December 1961–26 February 1994)*

I know he didn't die this year, but it's not only sad to remember that he's dead but also to realize that he was perhaps the one man who could have helped us through the endless fuckery of it all.

# General shittery: random shit awful stuff that's happened

## *The Euros*

Really?? Oh for fuck's sake! Not a-fucking-gain! Iceland????!!! You've got to be kidding me! A country with a population the size of Croydon, they said, as if the population of a country should be directly proportional to its footballing success. So, farewell then, Roy Hodgson. Don't underestimate the quiet man, said Iain Duncan Smith when he took the reins of the country. And didn't HE do well? To be fair, Roy seemed like a genuinely nice bloke – a seasoned gardener trying to make the best of an allotment that had gone to shit, and into which the neighbouring allotment owners had been dumping ordure. Well, never mind, look here! It's Big Sam! Hoorah! His honest-guv wheeler-dealer no-bullshit straight-talking tough-walking approach would kick us into shape, wouldn't it? Surely? But no, corruption got to him too, and after a painful newspaper sting he found himself out of a job. Still, he goes on record as the only England manager to not concede a single game. In fact he had a

100 per cent winning record. BECAUSE HE ONLY MANAGED US FOR ONE FUCKING GAME.

## The Orlando shooting

The deadliest mass shooting in US history. And an assault on diversity, inclusivity and acceptance. Just one of many truly awful terrorist attacks this year. FUCK YOU, 2016.

## Climate change

2016 may have made us feel like the human race is fucked, but it's always worth remembering that the planet we live on is fucked too. 2016 looks set to be the hottest year ever, the third record-breaking year in succession, which would mean that sixteen out of the seventeen hottest years in history have occurred this side of the new millennium.

So as the ice caps melt and we slide towards a *Day After Tomorrow*-style apocalypse, what does the newly-elected leader of the Free World think about this most pressing of issues? Luckily for us, Donald Trump's cavernous archive of bilge (a.k.a. his Twitter account) sheds light on the matter:

'*The concept of global warming was created by and for the Chinese in order to make US manufacturing non-competitive.*' (6 November 2012)

'*This very expensive GLOBAL WARMING bullshit has got to stop. Our planet is freezing, record low temps, and our GW scientists are stuck in ice.*' (2 January 2014)

Nice to know planet Earth is in safe hands, then.

## *Junior doctors*

It's not enough that they should devote their lives and careers to helping others, but clearly working ridiculous hours and not getting renumerated reasonably for them is required, too, thanks to the arsetrumpetry of Jeremy Hunt. Sorry – Jeremy fucking Hunt. On top of that, vilification in the press followed, just to cap it all. Next time Jeremy finds himself requiring complex surgery for having a large spanner removed from his arse, during NON-WORKING hours, let's see if he can find a junior doctor happy to help. Possibly not.

# The man-bun

bun

man

Man-bun or '*MUN*' – possibly the most unholy contraction in the English language since chillax. But not, we hasten to add, the first (and no doubt not the last) truly dire thing to happen to male grooming. Oh no, there's form on this. Come, as we take a whistle-stop tour of a grand heritage of irresponsible hair growth.

## The mullet.

the classic mullet

*An exceptional style that came into its own in the 80s, pretty much dominating an era not just for men's hair but for women's hair, too. Step back to an urban shopping centre circa 1984 and look around you; you'd be forgiven for thinking that, just based on hair growth alone, you were in the midst of a pretty shittastic year. The mullet has recently enjoyed something of a minor renaissance in the last year or so, but only amongst twats.*

## The Tudor bowl cut.

*the bowlcut*

*A strange and fundamentally ugly look. Combine it with a man bun and the universe might implode. Fortunately, this has never yet been attempted.*

## The mediaeval monk

*the medieval monk*

*The carefully cultivated bald patch, the bowl cut . . . all in all, a very sexy look. Yet one designed with an austere and reverential ambition of saving God a little bit of time working his way through the hair to reach the skull and brain of the acolyte to convey his divine messages. Because, you know, he must be in a REALLY big hurry most of the time.*

## Zika

Just terrible. FUCK YOU, 2016, YOU MASSIVE ARSE.

## Earthquakes

One would be too many, but we've *really* had too many this year, Italy and New Zealand among them. Earth reminding us that she really doesn't give a fuck, which is why we all *should*.

# THE BAKE-OFF FIASCO

This is an interesting one, because on the one hand we were distraught at the prospect of losing a beloved show from its rightful home on the BBC to a commercial channel; yet on the other hand, it showed an admirable and quite beautiful set of values from some (or, erm, three) of its presenters. Fuck the money, we're sticking with the BEEB. All hail Mary! And Mel and Sue, of course.

## Top Gear *in its new incarnation*

Fresh with the wonderful mental image of Jeremy Clarkson twatting someone in the face simply because they had served him a cold steak, we prepared ourselves for a new iteration of a show that relied entirely on the unique chemistry of its presenters. An immediate problem presented itself in the unique chemistry of the new presenters. Not least responsible among them was Eddie Jordan, whose personality shone with the blinding brilliance of wet cardboard.

## *Brangelina and Depp/Heard*

Does love even exist anymore?

## *Spiralizers, courgetti and budles*

To clarify: budles are noodles made out of butternut squash. Of course.

## *Hygge*

Britain is either grey, wet, dark, cold, raining, flooded, sleeting, cloudy, cold, cold or cold for 87 per cent of the year. Us Brits have, therefore, never needed any assistance or form of instruction on how to stay inside in the warmth. The publishing phenomenon of 2016 is the Danish art of *hygge*. Will it finally rid us of endless colouring-in books? What can we glean from this intolerably-difficult-to-pronounce-term-that-has-no-English-counterpart-but-essentially-just-means-cosy? Well, you could put on some socks. Sit down on a chair and knit. Make a warm beverage and drink it out of bowl instead of a mug. Arrange sticks and leaves delicately around your dining table for absolutely no reason. Wear a jumper and smile at your Aryan child. You could EVEN snuggle down by the fire with one of the 76890 *hygge* books on offer. The choices are endless.

## *Pokémon Go*

Some would say that anything that gets teenagers out and about and off their arses is a good thing. THEY WOULD BE WRONG. Pokemon Go is arguably the beginning. Of the end. The merging of reality and virtual reality that it offers, and the gamification it presents, are nothing if not troubling. What next? Will we see a version of Mortal Kombat hit our streets, with kids crying, 'finish him!', whilst attacking geriatric strangers? Let's hope not.

## *The Toblerone Travestry*

No! Really? Now? When the world is going to shit, they decide to REDUCE THE VOLUME OF TOBLERONE BARS BY INCREASING THE GAPS BETWEEN THE LITTLE CHOC-OLATE PYRAMIDS? Honestly, for fuck's sake! FUCK YOU, 2016 AND YOU CAN RAM A TOBLERONE UP YOUR ARSE WHILE YOU'RE AT IT.

## *Bono*

Named as one of Glamour magazine's Women of the Year. Surely a sign, if ever there was one, that there's something slightly surreal and bizarre about 2016.

## *That programme where you choose a potential partner based on their genitals – and, by extension, Anna Richardson*

Really? I'd be fascinated to know what John Reith might have made of this. Right at the inception of TV, at the launch of a bright new hope for educat-ing, unifying and enriching the cultural life of the nation, did Baron Reith conceive a week night evening show where people would be judged by their dongs?

## The Mannequin Challenge

Have we fallen so far as a society that we have turned from emulating reality TV stars made of plastic, to pretending to be mannequins made of the same mindless, soulless material? Most people do not have enough time to teach their children how to read, but they have plenty of time to gather a group of like-minded idiots to meet up at the pub and shoot a two-minute video of people frozen in a moment of their own mediocrity. All this to gain a simple thumbs-up on their favorite anti-social media plat-form they call a life. What makes matters worse is that celebrities have taken to this ill-thought-out trend to new heights. As if TV wasn't mindless enough! Now let's watch bullshit blathering hosts stand in place to fill the airtime that would be wasted on non-sense anyway. Now you get to watch this fucking balderdash frozen in time like that dog turd your neighbor so politely left on your lawn while he was performing The Mannequin Challenge on fucking humanity. Fuck you, 2016, for giving us this bullshit trend, and fuck you to all who have wasted time recording and watching it. We're better off relating to actual mannequins rather than those who are trying to imitate them. At least they are usually wearing something nice.*

## *Barbers that offer eyebrow threading*

Barbers that wha??

## *Sugar tax*

There are two views here. One being that childhood obesity is, to coin a now tired expression, reaching epidemic levels, and that increasing the tariff on sugary treats will price them out of the market. The other flip side is that it's a cleverly opportunistic taxation policy which will generate vast amounts of cash whilst being unassailably popularist and, therefore, 'a good thing'. But are we really so helpless that we need to be 'saved' like this? Saved from treating ourselves to something NICE? Why don't we just go for the full hog and have a fun tax?

* *Contributed by a friend in the US who is really, really annoyed about The Mannequin Challenge. If you bump into him, DON'T STAY STILL! KEEP MOVING!*

## 'Netflix and chill'

Netflix and fuck off.

## BHS

What does it profit a man if he gains a superyacht but remains a total nob-swab?

## Samsung exploding bomb phones

Erm . . . not ideal, really, is it?

## Russians doping at the Olympics

Depressing.

## The EpiPen pricing outrage

A nasty, grim reminder that rapacious greed can infil-trate everywhere in life, even into the world of life-saving medicines.

### Bob Dylan dissing the Nobel Prize committee (and refusing to attend the award ceremony)

Oh, just fuck off, Bob. Really? Accept the trophy you ungrateful arse!

### The horrifyingly hateful reactions to the Black Lives Matter movement in the US

Not to mention the horrifying number of black people who have been killed without cause by police this year.

### A 79-year-old Trump supporter who vandalized a kids' mural, writing over 'Make America Love Again' with 'Make America Great Again' as well as 'suck it up buttercup' and 'get over it cry babies'.

You fuckmuppet.

### Harambe the gorilla

Just an awful, tragic thing – a poor little boy climbs into a gorilla enclosure and into the hands of

Harambe, a 440-pound silverback, who was then shot out of fear for the boy's safety.

## The Marmite price hike

What a shitstorm of a fiasco this was. As if 2016 hadn't been bad enough already. They can take our dignity. They can take our pride. But try to touch our Marmite? Screw Pot Noodle, PG Tips, Vaseline (for those of you who saw red in the heat of the moment and forgot there were other brands that also got price-hiked). Marmite was the ticket. It's a bit mental that we, the British, who have literally ostracized an entire nation for its rejection of tea, suddenly couldn't care less about the price of tea, or shitty American-brand mayonnaise or I-can't-fucking-believe-it's-not-fucking-butter for that matter. No, what got our panties in a twist was Marmite. The. Last. Fucking. Straw. I know many of you were outraged. I was too. It was only after the whole fiasco died down a bit that I took stock of my panicked purchases. Fortunately, I now have eight decades' worth of Marmite. Love it or hate it indeed.

## Mulled wine scented toilet roll from Tesco

Why pass a stool on anything less?

## *Gary Lineker being vilified by tabloid media*

For being what? Decent? I love you, Gary. I think you're a hero. And not just for presenting *Match of the Day* in your underpants.

## *Cecil the lion*

Killed by a twat with a big gun. Who probably has a very small penis.

## *The Ryan Lochte Olympic lies*

Ryan! You nob! You're a sportsman! People look up to you! Don't be a twat!

## *Hiddleswift*

To be fair, Taylor Swift and Tom Hiddlestone's releationship kept most of us entertained for a good couple of months. Was it a couple of months? Lord knows. It was over pretty *swiftly*. Ha. Aha. Aha ha ha. The best thing about it was possibly those godawful photos that didn't look *at all* staged. Wait – hang on – they actually were? She hired a professional photographer to take pictures of them having fun?! Best of all was *that* one of Ryan Reynolds looking like someone's just told him he's going to spend the rest of the week having his rectum examined.

## The Orlando Bloom naked paddle boarding incident

No need, Orlando. There was simply no need for this. The world didn't need to see Legolas's cock.

## Post-truth

That this very concept exists is bad enough but that it characterizes our political landscape is terrifying. But it does, doesn't it? It's not the facts you express but how, and how forcefully, you express them. £350 million spent on the EU that could be redirected to the NHS? Barack Obama was the founder of Isis? Oh, wait, you mean that's just bullshit? Oh. Fuck. Too late! You had me!

This author blames Big Brother and the proliferation and reiteration of reality TV. The growing convergence of actual reality and constructed televisual narrative into 'dramality' – reality TV that's been enhanced for entertainment purposes – mean that we, the public, are getting used to fact as entertainment.

Fact just on its own isn't enough. How can it compete? Which is how a giant fuckmuppet like Trump can take power. How we laughed when he sent that first tweet, suggesting he knew which contestants might make it on to his new team! How reassuring to know he'd be treating governance of the Free World just like an inane reality show! Ha!

## Hashtaggery

Fun can also become dumb.

## Selfie sticks

How about just enjoying yourself and REMEM-BERING that you had a nice experience?

## People saying 'I know, right?'

Yes, I know. Believe me, I KNOW.

## People saying 'I can't even'.

What? You can't even what? Finish a sentence?

## *People using 'text' as a past participle — as in 'I text him yesterday'.*

No, you didn't, you fool.

## *The killer clown craze*

A bit lost for words on this one, as it slightly defies rationalizing or, conversely, satirizing. It begs the question, though, what next? Are we poised to see killer Teletubbies launching waves of attacks across Europe?

## *Those men boasting about surfing on a turtle*

I'd love to see a turtle shell shoved up your arses.

# Shit years throughout history

So, we've now waded through a non-exhaustive stinking quagmire of excrement, building a picture of this truly abominable year. But how can we really know just *how* terrible it's been unless we look to history to provide us with a sense of context? Surely there have been some other utter bastards of years in the past? Perhaps *even worse* than 2016? Follow me, reader, as we take a journey back through time to find out . . .

## *Circa 72,000 BC*

Around seventy-four thousand years ago, the precise date can remain vague, there was a very, very big fucking volcanic explosion, or rather a volcanic super-eruption, to use the correct term. The island of Sumatra in modern-day Indonesia was all but obliterated, as a mountain from which it sprang exploded with a force equivalent to 1.5 million Hiroshima-sized bombs. As if Earth had had a particularly bad night on the booze, complemented by a questionable kebab, her insides were projectile vomited to such a degree that rocks and magma travelled the distance of whole continents. As I said, this was a *BIG FUCKING VOLCANO*. Volcanic ash covered Asia and reached as far as Africa. Unsurprisingly, a geological shart of such proportions impacted on the global climate and, with the sun blocked out, temperatures plummeted. This long dark night of our planet's soul destroyed the food chain and the indications are that the HUMAN RACE WAS REDUCED TO LESS THAN 10,000 PEOPLE. That would be a fairly decent turnout for a Status Quo gig, then. The fact that the world population is now at around 7 billion can only indicate that, whatever the intervening years have brought us, a vast amount of shagging has gone on.

## *AD 79*

An incredibly crap year if you lived in Pompeii.

## *1066*

A shit-tsunami of a year for the English. Invaded by the Normans, with property distributed among their ruling classes, the shat-upon Anglo Saxons had very little to console themselves beyond the prospect of inheriting some better and less silly names for themselves. Soon, Aethelflaeda, Aedelnod, Hrothulf, Mildpryd, Sunngifu and Wigheard would be but a thing of the past . . .

## *1241*

The year the Mongols invaded Europe. Not a good year if you weren't a Mongol.

## *1348*

The Black Death was a bit of a downer, all things considered. In the space of just a year and a half it killed off over a third of the entire population of Europe, with an estimated total deaths at between 75–200 million . . . It took three centuries for the global population to return to its previous level. The plague appears to have begun somewhere in central Asia before passing along trade routes, carried by *oriental rat fleas*. As if it wasn't e-fucking-nough to get the plague, the final insult came from what delivered it.

So what was the plague? Was it *really* that bad? Well, erm, yes. First of all you'd get massive buboes the size of apples appearing on your body, centred around your groin, armpits and neck. These would be full of pus, naturally. After this onslaught of particularly bad acne, you'd develop a rather nasty fever and start coughing up blood. And then you'd DIE.

Much like us contending with the challenges of 2016, our counterparts in the fourteenth century looked, desperately, for reasons to explain this terrible fuck-tastrophe that they were facing. People thought, perhaps justifiably, that the end of the world was on its way . . . How to make amends? Well, for starters, sex was most definitely not on the menu: 'fleshly lust' was strictly to be avoided, not that this did much to help. A more extreme response was flagellating. That's whipping yourself, but not for fun. So many died that bodies littered the streets; families, towns and cities were decimated. In short, it was a truly fucking dreadful time. HOWEVER, there were upsides – the plague had the effect of reducing inequality, ending feudalism, and ushering in a period of free-thinking and humanism. So, not all bad.

## *1520*

Smallpox arrived in America, killing nearly 90 per cent of the indigenous population. A fucking horrendous year for the native Americans.

## *1596*

A consecutive series of really crap harvests in Britain fucked things up for all but the very rich. Around thirty thousand Londoners (the equivalent of a million people today) were forced out of their homes and on to the streets, begging for whatever they could find. The wages of an average worker dropped to two thirds of the level they'd been a hundred and fifty years previously. All of which perhaps puts our angst about present-day stock-market fluctuations into perspective.

## 1845

The first year of the Irish famine. An apocalyptically shit time for the Irish.

## 1848

The Irish famine reached its zenith of awfulness whilst revolutions took place across Europe, toppling the French monarchy.

## 1916

The First World War had already claimed a vast number of lives, but now conscription was introduced, income tax soared and zeppelins started bombing the shit out of England. And then, in July, came the Battle of the Somme – and over a million young men were killed in one of the most pointless moments in military history.

## 1919

The war was over and won, but in America things turned to shit. Inflation and unemployment went through the roof, whilst influenza wiped out half a million people. Race riots broke out across the nation. And to top things off, prohibition was introduced! People weren't even able to get arsebadgered beyond recognition to help ease the pain.

## 1943

Unlike the First World War, the Second World War is just about within in our popular memory, with its horrors and its consequences still reverberating and influencing us to the present day; and for those who didn't live through it, it's hard to imagine the terror and tragedy that it wrought on individuals, their families and their countries. 1943 was perhaps an apex of awfulness, as by then the Nazis had killed over 1.3 million Jews, with the Holocaust now fully underway. News of this may have been beginning to spread, yet no decisive and direct action took place. Further afield, to support the war effort and feed Britons and the British armed forces, there was a massive increase in food imports from British-run India. This prompted a famine in Bengal, which wiped out approximately 3 million people. Just one of many indirect and unanticipated consequences of a war that impacted on almost every living human being on the planet.

## 1968

Martin Luther King and JFK were assassinated, whilst Nixon came to power. Student revolts occured in France, prompting up to 9 million workers to join them and go on general strike, but President de Gaulle's show of military force within the country soon brings the movement to a standstill. Meanwhile, the Soviet Union invades Czechoslovakia, ending the 'Prague Spring' and enforcing 'normalization'.

## 1971

A prototype of the mullet is first trialled. Somewhere in Basingstoke, allegedly. The catastrophic consequences prompt those involved to destroy the blueprint. Several years will pass before it makes a return.

## *2001*

So much happened in the wake of 9/11 that it's hard to piece together a sense of events, let alone say anything cogent about its impact. But it's perhaps incontrovertibly true that without it having happened, much of the awfulness of the last fifteen years *wouldn't* have happened, or certainly wouldn't have happened in the same way – from Afghanistan and Iraq, the Arab Spring and Syria, to the present-day doubts and concerns over the functionality of Nato and the UN.

If this little section has depressed you, please accept the apologies of the author. If it shows anything, it's two things: firstly, that mankind is capable of being an absolute wank-bastard to itself but also, secondly, that we have enough wank-bastardry just contending with the stuff the universe throws at us, from earthquakes and volcanoes to famines and disease. You'd think the second would be sufficient to prevent us from having to bother with the first, wouldn't you?

# Did they really say that??

## *Trumpisms*

'You know I'm automatically attracted to beautiful — I just start kissing them. It's like a magnet. Just kiss. I don't even wait. And when you're a star, they let you do it. You can do anything. Grab them by the pussy. You can do anything.'

'That makes me smart.' Responding to the suggestion that he pays no income tax.

'You could see blood coming out of her eyes. Blood coming out of her wherever.'

'I'm building a wall.'

'I alone can fix it.'

'40 Wall Street actually was the second-tallest building in downtown Manhattan . . . And now it's the tallest.' Boasting about Trump Tower following the attack on the World Trade Center.

'Why can't we use nuclear weapons?'

'They don't write good. They have people over there, like Maggie Haberman and others, they don't – they don't write good. They don't know how to write good.' Attacking *The New York Times*

'[Putin] is not going into Ukraine, OK, just so you understand. He's not gonna go into Ukraine, all right? You can mark it down. You can put it down.'

## *Borisisms*

'Voting Tory will cause your wife to have bigger breasts and increase your chances of owning a BMW M3.'

'Despite looking a bit like Dobby the House Elf, he [Putin] is a ruthless and manipulative tyrant,'

In describing a visit that Tony Blair was making to the Congo, Johnson suggested Blair would be met 'with crowds of flag-waving piccaninnies' and that the 'tribal warriors will all break out in watermelon smiles.'

## *Faragisms*

'I think that politics needs a bit of spicing up.'

'The euro Titanic has now hit the iceberg – and there simply aren't enough lifeboats to go round.'

'We may have made one of the biggest and most stupid collective mistakes in history by getting so worried about global warming.'

'You know, I hear all these things about women's rights . . .'

# Tell me something good

Believe it or not, there's actually been some pretty good stuff that's happened in 2016. I know, not loads, but at least a few things worth mentioning.

For starters, apparently the average person earns three times as much as they did in 1966, making adjustments for inflation. They also live a third longer than before and IQs are higher everywhere. Wait!! What??? IQs are *higher*?? Explain what the fuck's been going on, then! That word *everywhere* needs some serious qualification. And let's ignore the fact that Brexit and all the other endless tomfoolery that's happened may really fuck about with what people earn. And how long they live. But yes, sorry, the general point being that some of these key indicators are actually heading upwards.

And despite impressions, there's 98 per cent less chance of dying from floods, storms or droughts than there was a hundred years ago.

A few other rather good things:

## The Queen

She celebrated her 90th birthday and made the country feel proud and happy for her. #stillalegend.

## Sadiq Khan

At last, a mayor of London who we can actually feel proud and optimistic about.

## Andy Murray winning at Wimbledon

Go Andy! It's almost hard to believe, such as his ongoing success, that we never really believed that the trophy could be won by a Briton. It may just be a game, but he's single-handedly managed to wipe out national gloom and pessimism, albeit in tennis. And that's pretty amazing, isn't it?

## Tim Peake successfully completed his ISS mission and came back from space

Go Tim! One of the loveliest things about him has been his genuine wonder at the universe, which we've all begun to share. And seeing him reunited with his family after being up in space for six months was just brill.

## *The Foreign Office got a new cat*

Enter Palmerston the 'diplocat'! Cats just have a positive effect, don't they? You could plop a cute Bengal with a name like Terry in a funeral parlour and it would immediately brighten things up. And lord knows that we've needed something to brighten up Westminster. (Let's ignore the existence of Cronus – a tarantula living in the office of the conservative chief whip, Gavin Williamson . . .)

## *Tiger numbers have risen for the first time in a century*

There are now apparently 3,890 wild tigers out there, up from 3,200 six years ago. Conservation exercises have been successful in a range of places, including India, Russia and Nepal.

## *Leicester City won the Premier League*

Whoever you support, you've got to admit, that was pretty fucking special.

## There are more manatees in the world!

Yes, manatees! You know the ones: large aquatic, mostly herbivorous marine mammals sometimes known as sea cows. Yes, them!

## Volunteers in India planted 50 million trees in twenty-four hours

Although the feat has yet to be certified by Guinness World Records, Indian officials have reported that volunteers planted a whopping 49.3 million tree saplings on 11 July, blowing past the previous record for most trees planted in a single day.

That record, a mere 847,275 trees, was set by Pakistan in 2013.

## Five hundred elephants are being relocated to safer home

A man-made migration, the largest elephant relocation ever attempted anywhere in Africa, is moving five hundred animals from a cramped park in Malawi.

## *Two hundred strangers attended the funeral of a homeless WWII veteran with no family*

Stating that 'in the military we don't serve alone, so we shouldn't die alone', Major Jaspen Boothe found out that only four people were attending the funeral of Serina Vine. She wasn't having that, so she posted about it online and word got out – and, happily, people came to pay their respects, giving Serina a proper send-off.

## *A four-year-old girl befriended a lonely, elderly man and helped him get over the pain of losing his wife*

On her birthday, little Norah Wood was out with her Mum, doing some shopping near home in Augusta, Georgia, when she spotted an elderly man on his own. She called out to him, told him it was her birthday and asked if she could have a photo with him. Obviously touched, he said yes and they had a chat. Norah was delighted with the new friend she'd made so she and her Mum decided to track the 82-year-old down in the hope of meeting him again. They managed to do so and, after visiting him and spending two and a half hours together, Norah soon became BFFs with 'Mr Dan'. It turned out that his wife had died earlier that year, leaving him alone and heartbroken. Making a new friend with Norah and her family was a good thing for all of them. Tara, Norah's mum, said the following about their meeting and the growing friendship: 'Sweet Mr. Dan is going to be part of our family whether he likes it or not (he likes it). Do yourselves a favour, friends – take the time to talk to older people. I think that sometimes we look right through them – like they're not even there. But you know what? They matter. They're valuable. They want to be seen and heard. They want to know they've not been forgotten. Let's take good care of them and love 'em all up.'

## *J. K. Rowling*

For loads of reasons, but most recently because she sent an ebook to a seven-year-old Syrian girl called Bana Alabed. Bana had watched a Harry Potter movie and loved it, so her mum tweeted Rowling to ask where she might be able to read one of them, given they had no easy access to the physical books. And hey presto! Or rather, 'Accio!'

# Will 2017 be less shit?

'Happiness depends upon ourselves' – Aristotle

Honestly, it could've been worse . . .

It's all too easy to find ourselves sitting up late each night with a bottle of grapefruit-flavoured vodka and a straw, ruminating on all the terrible things that have happened this year. It's easy to become despondent, listless, bad-tempered with our loved ones. It's easy to start wondering if people might be talking about us, whispering and laughing as we pass. It's easy to become preoccupied with thoughts of violence, thoughts of revenge . . .

But it's better, we think, to focus on the positives. Although there aren't any. Still, we should at least *try* to keep the negatives in some sort of perspective, don't you think? Yes, many heartbreaking, disappointing and horrifying things *have* happened this year – but shouldn't we take a moment to be thankful for all the appalling things that *didn't* happen?

When the vodka runs low and that dull ache in the centre of your forehead threatens to return, lift your spirits by reviewing the following helpful list . . .

*Editor's note: at the time of going to press several weeks of 2016 still remain. If, by the time you read this, any of the following have happened, please carefully cross out the relevant entries with a suitable marker pen.*

- A gigantic comet, asteroid or meteorite did *not* fall unheralded out of a clear blue sky, striking the surface of the Earth and putting a merciful end to what passes for 'life' on this Godforsaken planet.
- Despite their best efforts, a team led by Dr Fritz Lebenhass at the University of Dortmund did *not* conclusively prove that fresh air causes cancer.
- Canterbury Cathedral was *not* privatized and sold at a loss to an investment bank in Shanghai.
- Research by Dr Fritz Lebenhass (University of Dortmund) did *not* discover a clear causal link between Wi-Fi and male-pattern baldness.
- Or impotence (although he'll try again later).
- Great Britain did *not*, by a narrow margin in a referendum, vote to abolish nitrogen, Boyle's law or gravity.
- Sir Alan Sugar was *not* elected 45th President of the United States of America (despite losing the popular vote).
- At least three beloved popular entertainers, including, but not limited to, actors,

musicians and comedians, did *not* die (although see 'Editor's note', above).

- A race of 'carnivorous extra-terrestrial warthogs' (*'Fleischfressende extraterrestrische Warzenschweine'*) did *not* descend upon the Earth, devouring three tenths of the world's population in a fortnight, contrary to the predictions of Dr Lebenhass (*Zeitschrift fürunwahrscheinlich Prophezeiung* #292, p92).
- The Yellowstone Park Supervolcano did *not* . . . no, I'm not going to finish that.
- Er, that's it really. (Although, seriously, see 'Editor's note', above.)

*'Il faut cultiver notre jardin'* – Voltaire